HEALTHY COOKBOOK

Everyday recipes for your Thermomix

By

Lisa Wilson

Contents

Introduction

It happens to most of us: We have no time to cook, no motivation or we just don't have the required ingredients at home. So we eat what just happens to be in the fridge. Often we even eat standing in front of the fridge, just because we are so hungry and cannot wait for the food to be prepared!

This will not happen again with this book! You will prepare healthy and delicious dishes in record time with your Thermomix! The recipes are especially selected for busy people with a tight schedule who don't want to spend a lot of time cooking- But still want to eat healthy. Take the full advantage of your Thermomix – Stay fit and healthy using the recipes of this book.

Lisa Wilson presents multiple Everyday Recipes in this book. Besides main dishes you will find delicious recipes for salads, soups, smoothies and sweet desserts!

Carrot & Ginger Soup

INGREDIENTS

6 Portion(s)

- 30 g olive oil
- 400 g carrots, cut into large chunks
- 50 g onion
- 1 medium potato, peeled and cut in half
- 750 g water
- 2 heaped tsps. stock paste, or two cubes
- 10 g fresh ginger, peeled
- 1/2 tsp salt
- 1/4 tsp black pepper
- 6 wedges of lime

PREPARATION

1. Place olive oil, carrots, onion and potato into Thermomix jug.
2. Chop for 3 seconds/speed 5 and scrape the mixture down with spatula.
3. Add the water, stock paste (or cubes), ginger and salt/pepper.
4. Cook for 10 minutes/100°C/speed 2.
5. Blend for 1 minute/speed 6.
6. Serve with a wedge of lime and tortilla chips or crusty bread.

Miso Soup

4 portion(s)

- 500 g water
- 2 tbsps. Miso (white)
- 3 cm shallot, finely sliced
- 1/2 sheet Nori seaweed, finely shredded
- 60 g silken tofu, in 1cm cubes
- 1/2 tsp TM vegetable stock

PREPARATION

1. Bring water to boil for 5 minutes/100°C/speed 1.
2. Add tofu, seaweed, TM stock and miso.
3. Mix gently for 2 minutes/ 80°C.
4. Pour into small bowls and add a pinch of finely sliced shallots to garnish.

Thai Prawn Soup

INGREDIENTS

6 portion(s)

- 500 g cooked king prawns, peeled and cut in 3 pieces
- 1 stick lemongrass, cut in 3 pieces
- 20 g peeled ginger
- 100 g shallots
- 800 g coconut milk
- 200 g small mushrooms
- 35 g fish sauce
- 25 g lime juice
- 1 heaped tsp sugar
- to taste pepper
- 1 heaped tbsp. coriander

PREPARATION

1. Put the lemon grass, ginger, onion and coconut milk in a bowl.
2. Mix for 15 seconds/speed 7.
3. Then add the mushrooms, the fish sauce, the lime juice, the sugar and the pepper.
4. Mix for 15 minutes/100°C/speed 1.
5. Liquidize for 1 minute/speed 7.
6. Add the prawns and mix for 15 seconds in reverse function.

Tomato Soup

4 portion(s)

- 30 g olive oil
- 1 piece onion, peeled and quartered
- 200 g chopped tomatoes
- 800 g tin of tomatoes, diced
- 1 tbsp. vegetable stock
- 10 g balsamic vinegar
- 1 medium potato, peeled and diced
- freshly ground white pepper to taste
- 1/2 bunch fresh basil
- 200 g water

PREPARATION

1. Add onion and chop for 5 seconds/speed 5.
2. Add oil and cook for 3 minutes/100°C/speed 1.
3. Add tomatoes and chop for 5 seconds/speed 5.
4. Add water, stock, balsamic vinegar, salt, pepper, diced potato.
5. Cook for 12 minutes/100°C/speed 1.
6. Add fresh basil and blend the mixture for 40 seconds gradually increasing the speed to 10.
7. Serve with garlic bread.

Pumpkin & Coconut Soup

INGREDIENTS

1 liter(s)

- 1 medium pumpkin or Butternut squash, chopped 1" cubed or chop in batches for 4 seconds/speed 6
- 1 white onion, quartered
- 2.5 cm fresh ginger
- 1 chili, seeds removed
- 4-5 sprigs of Thyme
- 1 can coconut milk, or packet of coconut cream
- 1 tsp stock paste/powder or 1 cube
- Salt & Pepper
- breadfruit or Cooked sweet potato chunks, to taste, to garnish

PREPARATION

1. Place onion, chili, ginger, garlic and thyme in bowl and blitz for 3 seconds/speed 7. Scrape down the sides of the bowl.
2. Pour in 200 ml of water, and add salt, pumpkin and stock powder and cook for 20 minutes/100°C/speed 1 or until the pumpkin is cooked.
3. Use more water if you're using a carton of coconut cream.
4. Add the coconut milk and cook further for 5 minutes/100°C/speed 1.
5. Check seasoning, add pepper and blend for 1 minute initially at speed 9 but gradually increasing the speed to 9.
6. Add cooked chunks of breadfruit or sweet potato and serve (optional).

Creamy Spinach Soup

INGREDIENTS

4 portion(s)

- 1 onion
- 1 carrot
- 1 stick celery
- 200 g baby spinach
- 1 capsule vegetable stock pot
- 1/2 tsp. dried mixed herbs
- 1/2 tsp. coriander
- Salt to taste and pepper
- 500 g water
- 40 g soft cheese, medium fat

PREPARATION

1. Cut carrot, onion and celery into large chunks and put into bowl.
2. Chop the vegetables for 4 seconds/ speed 7, and then scrape down sides of bowl.
3. Add water, stock pot capsule, mixed herbs, coriander and pepper and salt to taste
4. Put baby spinach into Varoma, cover and put on the lid of TM bowl.
5. Cook for 15 minutes/Varoma temperature/speed 1.
6. Add steamed spinach and soft cheese to contents of bowl and blend for 1 minute/ speed 5 - 10.
7. Serve hot.

Chilled Pea & Avocado Soup

4 portion(s)

- 1 avocado, (ripe)
- 0.5 cucumber
- 300 g frozen peas
- 3 sprigs mint, leaves only
- 3 sprigs dill, leaves only
- 3 sprigs parsley, leaves only
- 600 g water, chilled
- Salt
- Black pepper
- 1 tsp runny honey
- 1 tsp smoked paprika, plus extra to garnish
- Extra virgin olive oil, to garnish

PREPARATION

1. Place all ingredients in the mixing bowl and blend for 1 minute/speed 9.
2. Pour the mixture into a bowl and sprinkle with paprika, and drizzle with olive oil.

Prawn & Mussel Chowder Soup

INGREDIENTS

4 portion(s)

- 100 g smoked pancetta
- 1 onion, quartered
- 2 sticks celery
- 2 cloves garlic
- 1/2 lemon, (Juice of)
- 1.5 l veg stock
- 300 g sweetcorn
- 200 g frozen mussels, defrosted
- 200 g Tiger prawns
- 1 bunch parsley, chopped
- 150 g double cream

PREPARATION

1. Sauté the bacon for 7 minutes/120°C.
2. Set the thermomixer at gentle stir setting or until the bacon begins to turn to brown. The time taken will depend on how fine the bacon is chopped.
3. Add the onions, garlic and celery and chop for 3 seconds/speed 5 and then cook for 5 minutes/100°C/speed 1.
4. Add the lemon juice and cook for 1 minute/100°C/speed 1.
5. Add the stock and sweetcorn and cook for 5 minutes/100°C/Counter-clockwise. Operate the thermomixer at gentle stir setting.
6. Add the mussels and prawns and cook for 7 minutes/100°C/Counter-clockwise. Operate the TM at gentle stir setting or until the fish is properly cooked.
7. Add the cream and parsley and serve with crusty bread

Potato & Butternut Squash Soup

INGREDIENTS

4 portion(s)

- 1000 g water
- 2 tbsp. stock, Chicken or Vegetable
- 100 g onions, Cut into quarters
- 350 g Butternut squash, cut in to small cubes
- 250 g potatoes, peeled & cut into small cubes
- 2 cloves garlic
- Bunch of coriander leaves
- Salt to taste & Pepper

PREPARATION

1. Add water and Stock into a mixing bowl.
2. Place Varoma into position, and then place Butternut Squash & Potatoes cubes into Varoma dish.
3. Next put the onion cubes & garlic cloves in the Varoma tray and steam for 35 minutes/Varoma/speed1.
4. Add 5 minutes if needed to ensure that the Butternut squash & potatoes are cooked & softened.
5. Place the Butternut Squash, Potatoes, Onions & garlic in the bowl and close the lid and mix for 2 minutes/speed 7.
6. Add Coriander leaves, Salt & Pepper in the bowl, then mix for 20 seconds/speed6.
7. Adjust Salt & Pepper to taste.

Mushroom Soup

4 portion(s)

- 500 g mushrooms, 250g sliced
- 50-60 g onion
- 50 g butter
- 1/2 lemon, juice
- 500 g water plus vegetable stock paste or cube
- 10 g parsley
- 50 g crème fraîche
- truffle oil, to serve
- salt and pepper, to season

PREPARATION

1. Place the 250 g of whole (unsliced) mushrooms into the bowl.
2. Weigh in the butter and onion and chop for 5 seconds/speed 4.
3. Scrape down the sides of the bowl and cook for 2 minutes/100°C/speed 2.
4. Add the lemon juice, water/stock, 1/4 tsp. salt and the parsley and blend for 30 seconds/ speed 5-10.
5. Cook for 8 minutes/100°C/speed 2.
6. Blend the mixture for 30 seconds/speed 8.
7. Add the crème fraiche and the sliced mushrooms to the bowl and cook for 4 minutes/90°C/speed 1 in reverse direction.
8. Taste and adjust seasoning.
9. Serve with a teaspoon of truffle oil in each bowl and, if desired, sprinkle some chopped parsley.

Herb, Cabbage & Mushroom Salad

INGREDIENTS

6 portion(s)

- 1 lime, zest & juice
- 100 g extra virgin olive oil
- 50 g light soy sauce
- 1 green chili, seeds removed
- 1 clove garlic
- 1 fresh ginger knob
- 100 g mushrooms, sliced, thinly
- 150 g red cabbage
- 150 g white cabbage
- 1/2 bunch Thai basil leaves
- 2 sprigs fresh dill
- 5 sprigs fresh mint
- 100 g red radishes
- Salt and cracked pepper, to taste

PREPARATION

1. Chop lime zest, garlic, ginger and chili for 10 seconds/speed 10.
2. Add the olive oil, soy & half the lime juice and mix for 5 seconds/speed 10.
3. Pour over the mushrooms to marinate.
4. Add the remaining ingredients to the TM bowl & chop for 2-3 seconds/speed 5.
5. Mix with the marinated mushrooms and serve straight away.

13

Beetroot & Carrot Salad with Feta & Pomegranate Molasses

INGREDIENTS

Dressing

- 20 g pomegranate molasses
- 20 g balsamic vinegar
- 45 g orange juice
- 30 g olive oil
- 1 tbsp. honey

Salad

- 400 g beetroot, peeled and quartered
- 400 g carrot, peeled and quartered
- 50 g raisins
- 20 g sunflower seeds, toasted
- 20 g pumpkin seeds, toasted
- 1/4 tsp salt
- Baby spinach leaves and feta to serve

PREPARATION

Dressing:

1. Place dressing ingredients into mixing bowl and mix for 5 seconds/speed 5.

Salad:

1. With dressing remaining in mixing bowl, add carrots and beetroot and chop for 4-5 seconds/speed5.
2. Spatula can be used to mix and ensure that all the ingredients are evenly chopped. Scrape down the sides of the bowl.

3. Add raisins, seeds and salt and combine for 3-4 seconds/counter-clockwise operation/speed 2.

4. Serve salad on baby spinach leaves and top with crumbled feta.

Chunky Coleslaw

8 portion(s)

- 1 carrot, roughly chopped
- 1/2 brown onion, quartered
- 1/4 cabbage, finely sliced
- 3 tbsps. mayonnaise
- 3 tbsps. Italian salad dressing
- 1 pinch of ground black pepper

PREPARATION

1. Add carrot and onion to bowl and chop for 3 seconds/speed 7.
2. Then scrape down the sides of the bowl and repeat if required.
3. Add sliced cabbage to the bowl. Mix on reverse at 5 seconds/speed 3.
4. Add mayonnaise, salad dressing and pepper and mix for 15 seconds/reverse/speed 3.
5. Serve immediately.

Spinach Salad

6 portion(s)

- 1 large handful young spinach leaves or silver beet, roughly chopped
- 1 small onion, peeled and quartered
- 1/2 red capsicum
- 130 g tomatoes, roughly chopped
- 100 g cup button mushrooms, wiped
- 2 tsps. sesame seeds, toasted
- 20 g olive oil
- 3-4 drops sesame oil
- 1/2 lemon, juiced (no pips)

PREPARATION

1. Put all ingredients, vegetables and dressing, into TM bowl and chop for 2-3 seconds/ speed 4.
2. Use spatula to scrape down and ensure all ingredients are chopped evenly and no large pieces remain.
3. If necessary, chop for a further 2 seconds/speed 4.
4. Do not over process salad.
5. Serve immediately.

Potato Salad

INGREDIENTS

8 portion(s)

- 1000 g red skinned potatoes
- 150 g diced bacon
- 2 spring onions, sliced
- 20 g olive oil
- 60 g parmesan, shaved
- 6 eggs
- 500 g water

Dressing

- 200 g mayonnaise
- 15 g wholegrain mustard
- 10 g balsamic vinegar

PREPARATION

1. Add bacon, oil and spring onion (keep a little for garnish) to bowl.
2. Cook the mix for 3 minutes/100°C/speed 1 on counter-clockwise operation.
3. Transfer this to the salad serving dish and set aside. No need to wash the bowl.
4. Add 500 g water to the bowl. Put diced potatoes in the Varoma dish (no tray) and steam for 15 minutes/speed 2
5. Insert basket into bowl, add 6 eggs and cover with a lid with potatoes in.
6. Cook further for 14 minutes/speed 2. Check if the potatoes are cooked.

7. Remove basket with a spatula. Put eggs into a sink or bowl of cold water to cool down and peel them. Quarter and slice the eggs. Empty steaming water from bowl and dry.
8. Add dressing ingredients and mix for 5 seconds/speed3.
9. Pour potatoes into the salad bowl (on top of bacon & onion mixture).
10. Add eggs and shaved parmesan (keep a little for garnish) on top.
11. Pour dressing from bowl over the salad and mix dressing through until combined.
12. Top with some spare spring onion or fresh chives and some of the shaved parmesan.
13. Refrigerate until cool and serve.

us Cous Salad

INGREDIENTS

4 portion(s)

Dressing

- 3 cloves garlic
- 60 g extra virgin olive oil, plus extra to taste
- 50 g red onion, cut to halves
- 1 tsp dried oregano
- 1/2 tsp ground cumin and cinnamon
- 1/4 tsp ground ginger and cayenne pepper
- 1 tsp grated lemon zest, no white pith
- 40 g lemon juice, plus extra to taste
- 3 sprigs fresh mint and parsley leaves
- to taste salt and pepper

Salad

- 800 g water
- 200 g Israeli cous cous
- 200 g red lentils
- 200 g cauliflower and Broccoli cut into 2/3 cm
- 250 g cherry tomatoes, halved
- 100 g Kalamata olives, pitted
- 30 g pine nuts
- 40 g pistachio nuts
- 40 g slivered almonds

PREPARATION

Dressing

1. Place the garlic into a bowl and chop for 3 seconds/speed 7, then add the oil and cook for 1 minute and 30 seconds/100°C/speed 1.
2. Add the onion, oregano, cumin, and cinnamon, ginger, cayenne, zest and lemon juice and chop for 3 seconds/speed 7.
3. Add the remaining herbs and combine for 10 seconds/speed 2 at reverse function.

Salad

1. Add the water into the bowl and place the basket in the bowl and weigh the cous cous and the lentils into the bowl.
2. Place the Varoma dish into position and weigh the broccoli and cauliflower into it. Secure the Varoma lid and steam for 9 minutes/Varoma/speed 2.
3. Set Varoma aside and stir the cous cous and lentils, then stir the broccoli and cauliflower. Place the Varoma back into position, and cook for 2-4 minutes/speed 2, or until the lentils are cooked as desired.
4. Remove the simmering basket with the aid of the spatula and rinse the cous cous and lentils under cold water. Set aside to drain.
5. Transfer the drained ingredients into a large bowl and add extra oil, lemon juice, salt and pepper to taste. Refrigerate before serving.

Beetroot & Carrot Salad

4 portion(s)

- 300 g carrots, peeled if not organic
- 180 g beetroot, washed, peeled and quartered
- 1/2 tsp. sweet paprika
- 1/4 tsp. cinnamon
- 1/8 tsp. ground cumin
- 1 pinch salt
- 1 pinch cayenne
- 1 lemon, juice only
- 2 tsp. raw Honey
- 60 g raisins
- mint leaves, (a large handful, washed)

PREPARATION

1. Place all the ingredients, except the raisins and mint into the TM bowl. Chop for 5 seconds/speed 5.
2. Check the consistency of the salad. Chop for another second or two if desired.
3. Add the raisins to the bowl and stir for 2 seconds/speed 4 in reverse direction.
4. Top the salad with fresh mint leaves just before serving.

Quinoa Salad

4 portion(s)

- 400 g Quinoa (washed)
- 1 tbsp. TM Veg stock concentrate
- 900 g water
- 3 cloves garlic
- 1/2 red onion
- Fresh parsley, good handful
- fresh coriander, good handful
- 1 Punnet of cherry tomatoes
- 1 small red capsicum
- Juice of 1/2 lemon
- 1 tbsp. orange juice
- 1 tbsp. Tamari soy sauce
- Juice of 1 lime
- 20 g extra virgin olive oil
- Fresh chilli to taste
- 1 cm fresh ginger

PREPARATION

1. Thoroughly rinse quinoa.
2. Add water and stock to the TM bowl. Pour quinoa into simmer basket and place into bowl.
3. Cook for 18 minutes/Varoma temperature/speed 3.
4. Once cooked, drain the remaining water and allow quinoa to cool down. Add quinoa to TM and put in the fridge to cool.
5. Place garlic, onion, parsley, coriander, ginger and chili into bowl and chop for 3 seconds/speed 7. Put into the TM with the quinoa.

6. Do not rinse the bowl. To make the dressing, add olive oil, lime juice, lemon juice, orange juice and tamari soy sauce to the TM bowl. Mix for 10 seconds/speed 6.
7. Chop cherry tomatoes in half and dice the capsicum and put on top of quinoa salad.
8. Mix the dressing when the salad is ready to be served.

Sushi Salad

6 portion(s)

- 900 g water
- 400 g Sushi Rice
- 2-3 spring onion/shallots, cut into pieces
- 2 carrots, cut into pieces
- 150 g smoked salmon
- 1-2 avocados, cut into cubes
- 1 cucumber, peeled and deseeded
- 1-2 cooked prawns, per serving (optional)
- 3 nori sheets
- 4 tbsps. sesame seeds, dry roasted (white or black)
- pickled pink ginger, for garnishing

Dressing

- 30 g mirin
- 30 g roasted sesame oil
- 40 g soy sauce
- 2 lemons, juice only
- 30 g rice wine vinegar
- 1-2 tsp wasabi paste
- 100 g mayonnaise

1. Place water into the mixing bowl and rice into basket.
2. Insert basket and cook rice for 15 minutes/Varoma/speed 2.
3. Remove and place into large serving bowl and let it cool.
4. Place spring onions and carrots into mixing bowl and chop for 4 seconds/speed 4. Add them to rice.

5. Add fish of choice, avocado, and diced cucumber and set aside.
6. Make the dressing and toss gently through salad.
7. Serve garnished with prawns, sprinkled with sesame seeds, shredded Nori sheets and pickled ginger.

Dressing Method;

1. Place all ingredients except mayonnaise into mixing bowl and blend for 10 seconds/speed 7.
2. Add mayonnaise and stir for 10 seconds/speed 3.
3. Serve immediately.

Seafood Salad

5 portion(s)

- 1000 g mixed seafood including salmon fillet, prawns, scallops and other white fish fillet of choice, chopped into even sized 3 cm pieces
- 1/2 red onion, sliced
- 2 avocados, stone removed and sliced
- fresh baby spinach or salad greens of choice

Chili Citrus Dressing

- 2 oranges, zest and juice
- 1 lemon, zest and juice
- 5 sprigs coriander leaves
- 3 sprigs Italian flat leaf parsley
- 4 spring onions
- 1 green chili
- 2 tbsps. sweet chili sauce
- 50 g fish sauce
- 150 g olive oil
- 1 dash rice wine vinegar
- Freshly ground black pepper & sea salt, to taste
- Raw sugar, to taste

Salad Dressing

1. Place citrus zest into a clean and dry TM bowl and grate for 20 seconds/speed 8.
2. Add herbs and chili and chop for 10 seconds/speed 7.

3. Add all remaining ingredients, set dial to closed lid position and use pulse mixture 2-3 times on Turbo.

Seafood Salad

1. Divide seafood between Varoma dish and tray.
2. Add 800g water into mixing bowl, place Varoma into position and cook for 25 minutes/Varoma/speed 1.
3. To prepare salad arrange the plate with salad greens, sliced onion and avocado.
4. Add steamed seafood and drizzle with dressing.

Creamy Garlic Prawns

INGREDIENTS

4 portion(s)

- 5 garlic cloves, peeled
- 80 g butter, cubed
- 50 g plain flour
- 1/2 tbsp. TM stock concentrate
- 250 g water
- 110 g pure cream
- 20 g white wine
- 1 tsp. Dijon mustard
- 500 g green prawns
- Salt and pepper to taste

PREPARATION

1. Chop the garlic for 3 seconds/speed 5 and scrape down side of bowl.
2. Add butter and sauté, for 3 minutes/100°C/speed 1.
3. Add flour, stock, water, cream, wine and mustard.
4. Mix for 5 seconds/speed 4, then cook for 2 minutes/Varoma/speed 1.
5. Add prawns and cook for 6 minutes/100°C/Counter-clockwise operation/Gentle stir setting.

Quinoa Fried Rice

INGREDIENTS

3 portion(s)

Quinoa

- 900 g water
- 100 g quinoa
- 20 g TM stock concentrate, optional

Mix

- 300 g peas and corn (frozen)
- 100 g chicken thigh (optional), chopped in 1 cm cubes.
- Additional veggies of choice, chopped into small pieces
- 3 eggs, beaten lightly
- 20 g low salt soy sauce
- Pepper to taste

PREPARATION

Quinoa

1. Place water and stock concentrate in a bowl
2. Add TM basket and pour in Quinoa.
3. Close TM lid and place Varoma on top (mc removed)

Mix

1. In the bottom of the Varoma, place peas and corn, chicken or extra veggies of choice.
2. Insert Varoma tray and line with baking paper and ensure the top side vents are not covered by the paper - this is to make sure that steam can circulate.

3. Place egg mixture onto paper lined Varoma tray and season with a little pepper if desired. Place lid on top of Varoma and cook for 17 minutes/Varoma/speed 3.
4. Roughly chop Omelets' mixture and tip into large bowl, add veggies and Quinoa drizzle with soy sauce and mix.

Prawn Risotto

6 portion(s)

- 2 carrots
- 1 stick celery
- 4 mushrooms
- 4 cloves garlic
- Parsley to taste
- 50 g olive oil
- 400 g rice,
- 2 tsps. TMX veggie stock
- 180 g cream cheese
- 900 g water
- 400 g prawns - uncooked
- 100 g white wine
- 140 g cream

PREPARATION

1. Put vegetables, garlic and parsley in TM processor and process for 5 seconds/speed 7.
2. Add oil and sauté for 3 minutes/100°C/speed 1.
3. Insert butterfly. Add wine and rice; cook for 2 minutes/100°C/reverse speed.
4. Add stock, cream cheese, and water (and prawns if still frozen).
5. Cook for 20 minutes/100°C/reverse speed with basket in place of measuring cup.
6. If prawns are completely thawed, add after 6 minutes.
7. Pour into TM and wait for 5 minutes, then serve.

Pea & Haloumi Fritters

INGREDIENTS

18 portion(s)

Fritters

- 250 g frozen peas, thawed
- 250 g Haloumi
- 2 eggs
- 70 g plain or spelt flour
- 1 tsp. baking powder
- 80 g milk
- Coconut oil/olive oil, for frying

Side

- Fresh salad
- Lemon wedge
- Dollop of Greek yoghurt

PREPARATION

1. Add all ingredients (except oil for frying) to TM bowl and combine while operating in reverse function for 15 seconds/speed 4, or until well combined.
2. Heat oil in a frypan and add a tablespoon of batter into pan. Fry for 1-2 minutes each side or until golden and brown.
3. Serve with fresh salad, lemon wedges and a dollop of yoghurt.

Salmon & Veggies

2 portion(s)

- 500 g water
- 2 Salmon steaks
- Lemon
- Vegetables of choice, e.g.: broccoli, capsicum, asparagus etc.

PREPARATION

1. Place 500g of water in a bowl.
2. Add salmon steaks to the bottom tier in the Varoma and drizzle lemon juice.
3. Add chopped vegetables to the top tier.
4. Steam for 20 minutes/speed 3-4.

Lamb Burgers

4 portion(s)

- 750 g grass fed lamb mince
- 65 g brown onion, quartered
- 1 bunch coriander or parsley
- 1 tbsp. paprika
- 1 heaped tsp cumin
- 1 tsp. coriander
- 1 level tsp. cinnamon
- 1 level tsp. turmeric
- salt and pepper
- 1 tbsp. oil, (Avocado, Coconut, Olive)

PREPARATION

1. Place quartered onion and herbs in the bowl and cook for 3 seconds/speed 5 and then scrape down with the spatula.
2. Add mince, spices, salt and pepper and process for 15-20 seconds/speed 3/Counter-clockwise operation.
3. Warm up the oil in a large frying pan, while shaping the mixture into 4 good size burgers.
4. Place the burgers in the pan and fry on one side till cooked half way up, then turn over and finish cooking them.

Garlic Prawns

4 portion(s)

- 1 bunches parsley leaves
- 4 cloves garlic, peeled
- 1 tsp. chili flakes, (or use fresh chili)
- 100 g olive oil, (or preferred oil)
- 1.5 tsps. paprika, sweet
- 1000 g prawns - uncooked, (weight with shells), then peel, devein but leave tails intact
- 1.5 tbsps. dry sherry

PREPARATION

1. Chop parsley in Thermomix for 3 seconds/speed 6.
2. Remove from bowl for garnishing cooked prawns, or you can leave in bowl and cook through if preferred.
3. Add garlic and chili in TM Bowl and chop for 3 seconds/speed 7.
4. Add oil and paprika into TM Bowl and heat for 5 minutes/speed 1.
5. Add prawns and cook for 3 minutes/speed 1 on counter-clockwise operation.
6. Add the Sherry and cook for 1 minute/speed 1.
7. Pour out and sprinkle chopped parsley and serve.

Chili Mussels

2 portion(s)

- 1000 g mussels, fresh, cleaned
- 1 clove garlic
- 1 onion, peeled & halved
- 140 g tomato paste
- 1 bottle tomato sauce, Passato Di Pomodoro
- 50 g oil
- 2 tbsps. chilies, fresh, or ground paste
- 1 tsp. oregano, flakes

PREPARATION

1. Chop garlic and onion for 3 seconds/speed 6.
2. Sauté with oil for 5 minutes/100°C
3. Add tomato paste, sauce, chili & oregano. Cook for 15 minutes/100°C/speed 2.
4. Put cleaned mussels into Varoma on top of sauce and cook at Varoma for 15 minutes/speed 2.
5. Pour mussels into big bowl and top with sauce.
6. Serve hot

Chicken Satay Wrap

INGREDIENTS

4 portion(s)

- 1 package Rye wraps
- 3 garlic cloves
- 2 tbsps. homemade peanut butter
- 1 tsp. tamari
- 1 tsp. fresh lime juice
- 1 small red chili, de-seeded and finely chopped
- 1/4 cup of water
- 2 Cups of green cabbage
- 1 Cup of bean sprouts
- 340 g skinless chicken breast, trimmed fat and shredded
- 2 medium tomatoes
- cracked pepper, to taste
- Himalayan pink salt, to taste
- 2 tbsps. coconut oil satay wrap

PREPARATION

1. Add garlic and chili to the bowl having closed lid for 4 seconds/speed 6;
2. Add peanut butter, tamari, lime juice, and water to TM, and process for 60 seconds/speed 7. Set aside.
3. Chop cabbage into chunks and add to the bowl and shred for 4 seconds/speed 5.
4. Add the sauce back into the bowl and mix for 10 seconds/speed 1/Counter-clockwise operation. Set aside.
5. Slice tomatoes to your desired liking and set them aside.
6. In a fry pan, add coconut oil.
7. Slice chicken into strips about 1cm thick and cook until golden brown.

8. Add the chicken, tomatoes and the cabbage salad to rye wrap.
9. Season with pepper and salt.

INGREDIENTS

4 portion(s)

- 500 g chicken breast, cubed 2cm
- 1 brown onion - large, cut into eighths
- 2 cloves garlic
- 30 g olive oil
- 3 tsps. chili paste with soya bean oil, heaped spoons
- 100 g oyster sauce
- 50 g light soy sauce
- 50 g raw sugar
- 100 g roasted cashews
- 1 shallots, to garnish

PREPARATION

1. Place garlic into TM bowl and chop for 3 seconds/speed 7.
2. Add oil and sauté at 2 minutes/100°C/speed 2.
3. Add chicken and cook for 2 minutes/Varoma/ counter-clockwise operation/gentle stir setting.
4. Add chili paste and cook for 2 minutes/Varoma/counter-clockwise operation.
5. Add oyster sauce, light soy sauce, raw sugar and onion cook for 5 minutes/Varoma/ counter-clockwise operation.
6. Add roasted cashews and cook for 1 minute/Varoma/counter-clockwise operation/Gentle stir setting.
7. Serve with rice and garnish with chopped shallots.

Caramel Banana Smoothie

INGREDIENTS

1 portion(s)

- 1 frozen banana
- 250 g soy milk (or milk of your choice)
- 2 deseeded dates
- 1/4 tsp. vanilla extract
- 4 Ice cubes
- sprinkle of cinnamon

PREPARATION

1. Add all ingredients to TM, close lid bowl and mix for 30 seconds/speed 9.

Protein Breakfast Smoothie

1 portion(s)

- 20 g almonds
- 30 g oats
- 1 scoop protein powder
- 1/2 banana, or 1 small banana (can be frozen or not)
- 150 g strawberries, hulled and frozen
- 250 g water, or milk of choice
- 50 g natural yoghurt
- 1 tbsp. chai seeds

PREPARATION

1. Ground almonds and oats for 30 seconds/speed 10.
2. Add remaining ingredients and process for 30 seconds/speed 8.

Breakfast Smoothie

INGREDIENTS

2 portion(s)

- 2 bananas, peel and break into 3 pieces
- 360 g unsweetened almond milk
- 50 g whey protein powder
- 40 g chia seeds

PREPARATION

1. Blend all ingredients in the mixing bowl and blend for 30 seconds/speed 4.

Lime & Avocado Smoothie

INGREDIENTS

1 portion(s)

- 1 lime (juice of)
- 80 g 0% fat Greek yoghurt
- 60 g raspberries (frozen or fresh)
- 1/2 avocado
- 10 g coconut oil
- 250 g almond milk
- 30 g protein powder

PREPARATION

1. Blitz all ingredients in TM jug for 60 seconds/speed8 and serve.

Ginger Smoothie

2 portion(s)

- 1 inch piece ginger fresh
- handful of dates
- Ice
- 1 banana
- Cinnamon to taste
- 700 g coconut water

PREPARATION

1. Add ginger and dates to a bowl with ice and mix on speed 9 or until finely chopped.
2. Add banana, cinnamon and coconut water to bowl and continue to mix on speed 9 or until the mixture is smooth.

Wake Me Up Smoothie

1 portion(s)

- 1 tbsp. raw organic honey
- 1 tbsp. Raw cocoa powder
- 1 tbsp. chia seeds
- 1 tbsp. organic coconut oil
- 1 tbsp. raw greens powder
- 1 tbsp. protein powder
- 1 banana, optional
- 1 portion fruit/veg to taste (optional)
- 100 g water, or add to consistency required

PREPARATION

1. Add all ingredients except the banana and mill for 30 seconds/speed 9.
2. Scrape bottom and sides of the bowl and add banana or any other fruit/veg desired.
3. Mix for 30 seconds/speed 9.
4. Add water to taste and mix for 10 seconds/speed 5.

Banana, Almond & Honey Power Smoothie

2 portion(s)

- 50 g raw almonds
- 500 g whole milk or milk of choice
- 1 tbsp. honey
- 2 bananas
- 100 g natural Yoghurt
- 1/4 tsp. ground cinnamon

PREPARATION

1. Place almonds in bowl and mill for 20 seconds/speed 9.
2. Place all remaining ingredients in bowl and mix for 1 minute/speed 9.
3. Serve and enjoy!

Green Smoothie

INGREDIENTS

2 portion(s)

- 2 lemons, - peel and pith removed
- 2 oranges, - peel and pith removed
- 2 mandarins, - peeled
- Ice blocks
- Water
- Kale - raw
- Sweetener to taste (optional)

PREPARATION

1. Add peeled fruit to TM bowl.
2. Fill a large glass (approx. 400-500ml capacity) with ice blocks and top it up with water.
3. Then add kale and blend for 1.5 -2 minutes/speed 8-9.
4. Taste before adding sweetener, and add according to the taste.
5. The sweetness will vary depending on the size of the lemons or mandarins/oranges.

Pomegranate & Strawberry Smoothie

2 portion(s)

- 1 pomegranate, (seeds only)
- 250 g strawberries, (fresh or frozen)
- 100 g red grapes
- 250 g ice cubes
- Water, not necessary if thick consistency is required
- Baby spinach, a good handful (optional)

PREPARATION

1. Add ice to clean bowl. Crush for 10-20 seconds/speed 9 or until there are no more chunks of ice.
2. Add rest of ingredients and mix for 30 seconds/speed 9 or until smooth.

Strawberry & Banana Smoothie

INGREDIENTS

4 portion(s)

- 300 g low fat milk, or lite soy
- 200 g ice cube, one average tray ice
- 2 bananas
- 125 g strawberries, fresh or frozen
- 200 low fat vanilla yoghurt
- 1 tbsp. oat bran or lecithin meal

PREPARATION

1. Place fruit in TM bowl and mix for 10 seconds/speed 4.
2. Place yoghurt, milk, ice and oat bran into the bowl and blend for 1 minute/speed 10.

Fruit ice cream

INGREDIENTS

8 portion(s)

- 400g of frozen fruit, for example raspberries or strawberries
- 2 egg whites (fresh)
- 100g of milk
- 2 tablespoons of liquid sweetener

PREPARATION

1. Add fruit to mixing bowl
2. Chop for 20 seconds / speed 10
3. Add egg whites, milk and liquid sweetener
4. Stir for 10 seconds / speed 6
5. Move the Ingredients to one side with the help of the spatula to be able to connect the mixer
6. Place the mixer and Mix for 2 minutes / speed until creamy and serve immediately

Apple & Lemon Zest Sorbet

2 liter(s)

- Zest 1 lemon
- 300 g apples, roughly chopped
- 700 g Ice cubes
- 2 egg whites

PREPARATION

1. Place lemon, apples, 350g ice and egg whites and blend for 8 - 10 seconds/speed 10.
2. Add remaining ice (350g) and, using spatula continue to blending for 1 - 2 minutes/speed 10, or until fruit and ice are incorporated.
3. Serve immediately.

Banana ice cream with basil

4 portion(s)

- 300g of mature frozen banana
- 10 fresh basil leaves
- ½ lemon zest
- 1 ripe banana (in pieces)

1. Add frozen banana in chunks, basil leaves and lemon zest in the mixing bowl.
2. Chop for 10 seconds / speed 10.
3. Add the ripe banana.
4. Mix for 5 seconds / speed 6.
5. Serve immediately.

Strawberry milkshake

INGREDIENTS

2 portion(s)

- 150g of frozen strawberries
- 600g of cold milk
- 1 trickle of liquid sweetener

PREPARATION

1. Add frozen strawberries into the mixing bowl.
2. Chop for 30 seconds / speed 10.
3. Push Ingredients down with the help of spatula.
4. Add cold milk and liquid sweetener.
5. Mix for 20 seconds / speed 10.

Dairy Free Chocolate Mousse

4 portion(s)

- 3 egg whites, (medium eggs)
- 30 g caster sugar
- 100 g dark chocolate chips, Callebaut or similar
- 30 g mild olive oil
- 2 egg yolks, (medium eggs)
- 1 tbsp. espresso Coffee

PREPARATION

1. Place egg whites in the bowl and whisk for 3 minutes/speed 2 for the first 2 minutes and increase the speed to 3 in the last minute. As the meringue is forming add the sugar to have a gloss. Set aside in a bowl big enough for the rest of ingredients.
2. Remove butterfly whisk and without cleaning the bowl, melt chocolate and olive oil for 2 minutes/50°C/ speed 0.5. Set on a different bowl.
3. Return butterfly whisk to the bowl and without cleaning it, whisk egg yolks for 2 minutes /37°C/speed 2.5.
4. Add chocolate and coffee and mix for 10 seconds/speed 2 and loosen the mixture with a 1/3 of the egg white and mix for 5 seconds/speed 2.
5. Remove butterfly whisk and add the chocolate mixture to the egg whites and very carefully incorporate both with the aid of a spatula.
6. Put mousse into a piping or freezer bag, cut the tip and pipe into glasses or ramekins. Rest in fridge until ready to serve.

Yogurt ice cream

2 portion(s)

Yogurt ice cream

- 250g of natural yogurt
- 1 tablespoon of sugared vanilla
- 1 teaspoon of honey

Strawberry sauce

- 100g of strawberries, natural, frozen or thawed
- 1 teaspoon of vanilla sugar
- 1 teaspoon of lemon juice

PREPARATION

YOGURT ICE CREAM

1. Add the ingredients for the ice cream in the mixing bowl
2. Stir to make creamy for 5 minutes / speed 4
3. Introduce the yogurt into the ice cream maker for 30 minutes
4. If you do not have an ice cream maker: Put the yogurt in a freezer bag and put it in the freezer for 30 minutes, knead it once and put it back into the freezer. After 3 hours it will be ready.

Strawberry sauce

1. Puree the strawberries with sugared vanilla and lemon juice for 30 seconds / speed 8
2. Pour in a glass one layer of frozen yogurt and one layer of sauce and so on till full
3. Decorate with fresh fruit or chocolate shavings

Raspberry ice cream

3 portion(s)

- 300g of ultra-frozen raspberries without added sugars
- 200g of cottage cheese

PREPARATION

1. Add ultra-frozen raspberries and cottage cheese in the mixing bowl
2. Mix all ingredients for 20 seconds / speed 6

Healthy Cookie Bites

INGREDIENTS

10 piece(s)

- 100 g rolled oats
- 1 banana, small and ripe
- 20 g maple syrup, or honey
- 30 g butter
- 1 tsp. vanilla extract
- 1 pinch cinnamon, optional
- 50 g chocolate chips, milk, white or dark

PREPARATION

1. Blitz the oats for 2 seconds/ speed 6.
2. Add the rest of the ingredients, except the chocolate chips and mix for 10 seconds/speed 4 to bring it all together.
3. Add the chocolate chips and mix on gentle stir setting for 10 seconds.
4. Transfer to a container or bowl and leave in the fridge or bench for 10 minutes.
5. Roll into balls.

Fruit salad with raspberry yogurt

4 portion(s)

Fruit salad

- 1 apple
- 1 pear
- The juice from 1 orange
- 1 banana

Raspberry yogurt

- 125g of raspberries
- 375g of yogurt
- 2 teaspoons of vanilla sugar

Fruit salad

1. Cut 4 apples and pears
2. Add the juice of an orange in the mixing bowls
3. Chop for 3 seconds / speed 4
4. Add the banana
5. Chop for 2 seconds / speed 4
6. Empty the content in a separate bowl
7. Clean and dry the mixing bowl

Raspberry yogurt

8. Add the raspberries to the mixing bowl
9. Chop for 10 seconds / speed 8
10. Add the yogurt and sugar vanilla
11. Stir for 30 seconds / speed 4
12. Serve raspberry yogurt over fruit salad

Organic Cacao Balls

INGREDIENTS

10 piece(s)

- 110 g almonds raw, nuts
- 110 g pitted dates
- 45 g coconut oil
- 35 g desiccated Coconut
- 30 g raw organic cacao powder
- 1 tbsp. chia seeds

PREPARATION

1. Place almonds into a TM bowl and chop for 20 seconds/speed 9.
2. Place all other ingredients together into TM bowl and chop for 20 seconds/speed 9.
3. Roll the mixture into bite sized balls and cover in desiccated coconut.

All the recipes and information in this book were carefully crafted. I strive hard to keep all the content as updated as possible. Nonetheless, it is impossible to avoid flaws or imperfections, therefore, I cannot offer any guarantee of accuracy, timeliness, quality, or integrity of the contents of the book. The texts and images are protected by copyright. Any publication, both in whole or in part, is strictly prohibited and requires the express permission of the publisher. The offense has legal consequences. Neither the publisher nor the author responds to the damage to the devices.

Printed:

Lisa Wilson

August 2017

Made in the USA
Middletown, DE
05 December 2019